Printed in the United States of America

PREFACE

This handbook of more than 200 activities and suggested songs has been developed to provide a resource for the many early childhood and elementary teachers who are serving children with a variety of special needs in inclusive and more restrictive settings. Children of all ability levels will enjoy these activities, but most importantly, children with developmental delays will derive the greatest benefit from them. Each activity has been carefully selected to promote specific types of development in areas where many children are deficient.

Equilibrium

The development of equilibrium is critical to maintaining one's balance while rolling, crawling, creeping, walking, running, jumping, hopping, and skipping. Anytime a child moves his/her center of gravity beyond the base of support equilibrium reactions cause automatic posture adjustments so the child does not fall over. The activities included in this section have been selected to ensure that children develop these critical reactions in a fun way.

Sensory Stimulation/Sensory Discrimination

For children to learn to discriminate among different types of touch, body movements, sounds, and sights, it is necessary for them to experience a variety of these sensations. For activities included in this section are designed to stimulate the tactile, proprioceptive, auditory, and visual systems.

Body Image

A well-developed body image helps children to understand their movement capabilities. The activities in this section help children identify their individual body parts, develop a whole body concept, and practice using their body in a variety of ways.

Basic Locomotor Skills
Mastery of basic locomotor patterns is required before a child can participate successfully in leisure, recreation, and sport activities. An efficient mover has learned to vary his/her locomotor patterns according to the demands of the environment. The activities in this section provide children the opportunity to practice modifying the force and flow of their movements through space.

Cross-lateral Integration
Cross-lateral integration is the ability to coordinate the two sides of the body during movement. Until this type of integration develops, children tend to use each side of the body independently and have problems with any activities requiring the use of their limbs at or across the midline (center) of the body. The activities in this section require the child to continually move beyond the midline.

Aerobic Fitness
Cardiovascular endurance is a critical component of a healthy lifestyle. The activities included in this section focus on aerobic exercises that will enhance cardiovascular endurance. The activities are particularly useful for in-seat, in-circle activities.

Use music whenever possible to enhance the experience. if possible, allow the children to choose the music, their contemporary, cultural-based music.

Animal Actions
Animal actions are fun ways to help children identify with a variety of animals, as well as develop their equilibrium, flexibility, strength/fitness and body image.

Cooperative Games

Cooperative games are included to enable children with a variety of abilities to work together to achieve a common goal. Participation in these types of activities help children to understand that every person has something to contribute to the success of a group.

We hope this handbook proves to be a useful tool which you will often refer to and utilize. We encourage you to contact us or our publisher, Mosby-Year Book, with any comments or suggestions for improvement. We also welcome your input concerning our text *Principles and Methods of Adapted Physical Education and Recreation, seventh edition*, for which this resource is a companion.

Carol Huettig
Jean Pyfer
David Auxter

TABLE OF CONTENTS

EQUILIBRIUM

Supine Equilibrium

#1

Turtle Stuck on Back

Ask the child to lie on his/her back and pretend to struggle to roll over, alternately flexing/extending arms and legs. Throughout, the head should be tucked to chest. When the child "struggles" hard enough, the teacher can help roll the turtle onto his/her stomach. Read a story about a turtle or, better still, let them watch a turtle who is stuck on his back.

Supine Equilibrium

#2

Protect the Pearl

Place a bean bag or "koosch" ball on the child's tummy. Ask the child to lie on his/her back until the "robber" tries to steal the "pearl." To keep from losing the pearl, the child should "tuck" according to ability. For example, one child may just tuck the chin to protect the pearl, while another is asked to tuck into a ball.

Supine Equilibrium

#3

Balloon Bobble

While lying on his/her back, with head tucked to chest, ask the child to keep a balloon up in the air, using hands, feet, elbows, knees, etc. A punchball may be used if the child is unable to make contact with the balloon. It may be necessary for the teacher to bounce the balloon off the child's body. The intent is to get the child to tuck chin and, if possible, lift shoulders off the ground.

Supine Equilibrium
#4
Group Balloon/Beachball Bobble

Ask a group of children to lie on their backs, putting feet into the center of the circle. The children, as a group, keep the balloon/beachball up in the air using hands and elbows. Then, modify the activity and ask the child to use feet and knees to keep the balloon/beachball in the air.

Supine Equilibrium
#5
Supine Scooter Play

Any supine scooter activity should be done with the chin tucked. Note: at first, if possible, use a scooter which supports most of the child's body; as the child develops more muscle tonus, the size of the scooter can be reduced.

Puppy on a Leash

Ask the child to lie on his/her back on a scooterboard, holding one end of a rope. Pull the child about the room.

Supine Equilibrium
#6
Pull Over the River

Suspend a rope over the child 2' from the ground. Ask the child to pull him/herself the length of the rope, head first, while lying on his/her back on the scooterboard.

Prone Equilibrium
#7
Superboy/Supergirl

Ask the child to lie on his/her stomach on a scooterboard and, holding arms and head up in air, glide down an incline or glide after 'blast-off"—the teacher's push.

Prone Equilibrium
#8
Peeking Turtle

The child lies prone, chin tucked to neck, with head covered by a "shell" (blanket, small mat, big bean bag) and then peeks out from under the mat or blanket, by lifting head. Reverse action, then, by having the child pretend s/he saw something scary, and tuck head to return to position "in shell."

Prone Equilibrium
#9
Alligator Pit

Ask the children to lie on their stomachs within a defined area. Ask one child to be the "hungry" alligator. On cue, the "hungry" alligator tries to "bite" the others (using hands/arms extended and clapping together to simulate biting action); each "bitten" alligator then becomes a "hungry" alligator, too, until all have been "bitten." Note: This activity can be done on scooters, as well.

Prone Equilibrium
#10
Sneaky Snake

Ask the children to lie on the floor (or scooter) at one end of the playing area. Call the child's name and then repeat the poem—

Here comes a snake,
Crawling up on me.
A long, thin wiggly,
------------------- snake I see!
(Child's name)

Prone Equilibrium
#11
Creepy, Crawly Worms

Sing "Creepy Crawly Worms" to the tune of "Ten Little Indians." Ask the child to crawl on stomach on floor, or on scooter.

Little worms are crawling, crawling,
Little worms are crawling, crawling,
Little worms are crawling, crawling,
crawling all around.

Little worms are playing, playing,
Little worms are playing, playing,
Little worms are playing, playing,
playing all around.

Prone Equilibrium
#12
"Peter Pan" Crocodile Clock

Read the story of "Peter Pan." Then, recite the following poem while the children crawl on the floor.

Crocodile, crocodile, tick, tick, tock,
Crocodile, crocodile, swallowed a clock,
Crocodile, crocodile, crawls around,
Crocodile, crocodile, down on the ground.

Prone Equilibrium
#13
Clapping Seal

The child pulls his lower body along the floor, while supporting his/her body in a push-up position. Occasional stops to rock and "clap fins" and make a seal "honk" make this a great deal more fun. If the child is unable to support self in this position, the child's chest could be supported by a bolster or pillow.

Prone Equilibrium
#14
Wheelbarrel Walk

Supporting part of the child's body weight on a bolster or rolled mat, ask the child to walk on his/her hands while the teacher holds the child just above the knees.

Sitting Equilibrium
#15
Sitting Tug of War

Ask two children to sit on the floor, facing each other, and play "tug of war" with a ball or heavy-duty balloon. Modify the activity by asking the children to sit on a rolled mat or on pillows while playing "tug of war."

Sitting Equilibrium
#16
Sitting Bounce

Ask a child to sit on a mini-trampoline, mat-covered tire, or a large ball while holding teacher's hands. The teacher should move his/her hands so that the child is forced into "disequilibrium" and must regain upright, sitting position.

Sitting Equilibrium
#17
Sitting Scooter Activities

Involve the child in any scooter activity which requires the child to sit on the scooter when moving.

Hands and Knees Equilibrium
#18
Robin Hood

Ask a child to assume an all-fours position next to another child, each facing the opposite direction. Shifting weight, each child should attempt to push the other child off balance.

Hands and Knees Equilibrium
#19
Ball Straddle

Ask the child to lie over the top of a big playground ball, keeping hands and knees in contact with the ground. Ask the child to lift hands and knees, individually at first and then two at a time, off the ground. The goal is to lie over the ball with no contact with the ground.

Hands and Knees Equilibrium
#20
Angry Cat

The child assumes an all-fours position on the floor. Then, hissing loudly, the child presses his/her back up to form an arch. Ask the child to hold the position for several seconds, while hissing. Then, ask the child to relax. This can be turned into a game by having one child be a "mean do" and alternately move close to and far away from the "cats."

Hands and Knees Equilibrium
#21
Dinosaur Walk

The child moves on all-fours, using opposite sides of the body alternately. The child moves the right hand and left knee forward together and then the left hand and left leg forward together (homolateral movement). Sing a poem to the tune of "Frere Jacques."

Brontosaurus, brontosaurus, Big and strong,
Big and strong.
Hold your head up high, Hold your head up high,
Move along, move along.

Hands and Knees Equilibrium
#22
Smart Dog

The child moves on all-fours, contralaterally. The child moves the right hand and left knee forward together; then the child moves the left hand and the right knee forward together (contralateral movement).

Hands and Knees Equilibrium
#23
Creepy Crawly Spider

Ask the children to creep about the room, while you sing (and they sing) the Creepy Spider poem to the tune "Eensy Weensy Spider."

The creepy, crawly spider is crawling cross the floor,
Creeping, creeping, crawling—crawling more and more.
Spider, spider, spider... where'd you go today?
Spider, spider, spider crawling all the way.

Hands and Knees Equilibrium
#24
Puppy with a Sore Paw

The child starts on all fours and then moves using both hands and one foot or one hand and both feet. Encourage the child to experiment with redistribution of weight necessary to make movement adjustments. Encourage the child to move forward, backward, and sideways.

Kneeling Equilibrium
#25
Mirror

Ask two children to face each other, while kneeling on a mat or carpet. Have one child move while the other mirrors the motion—the child who initiates the motion tries to "fake out" the partner and cause him/her to lose balance. There should be no physical contact between the children. At first, the teacher may have to be each child's partner in turn.

Kneeling Equilibrium
#26
Mirror with Contact

Ask two children to face each other and place hands together so that palms are touching. Using pressure on the palms, ask children to try to "push" over the other. Encourage the children to fake and move away from the upright position.

Kneeling Equilibrium
#27
Pillow "Fight"

Ask two children to kneel on mat and using pillows, try to push each other off balance. As the children get better at the above activities, repeat, but have the child kneel on one knee throughout.

Standing Equilibrium
#28
Standing Balances

Ask the child to stand on one foot with support/no support.
Ask the child to stand on one foot with hands on hips.
Ask the child to stand on one foot with hands above the head.
Ask the child to stand on one foot holding a ball over the head.
Ask the child to stand on a surface that "gives."

Standing Equilibrium
#29
Ostrich

Ask the child to stand on one foot while you recite the following poem. Ask the child to alternate feet.

Silly bird, silly bird,
One foot down.
Silly bird, silly bird,
Don't fall down!

General Equilibrium Activity
#30
Magic Carpet Ride

Ask the child to assume one of the following positions—supine, prone, sitting, hands and knees, or knee stand—on a mat, blanket, or quilt. Grasp the edge of the mat and "pull" the child about as if on a magic carpet ride. Change the dynamics of the activity by changing the site of the grasp. This activity can be incorporated beautifully into "classroom" activities that involve "travel."

General Equilibrium Activity
#31
Crazy Sidewalk

Place objects under a series of mats, so that the surface of the mat is lumpy, uneven and variable (bean bag chairs are great). Ask the child to perform locomotor activities on this surface—roll, crawl, creep, knee walk, walk, run, and each of the above "backwards."

SENSORY STIMULATION AND DISCRIMINATION

Tactile Activities

#32

Partner Massage

Teach children to give each other a massage as part of your stress reduction program. Introduce light touch and then deep pressure along the long bones of the body. When applying deep pressure, the child should use the fleshy part of the thumbs to stroke the length of the major muscle groups.

Tactile Activities

#33

Texture Rub

Rub the child with materials that have different textures: silk feathers, sponges, brushes, animal fur (fake), flannel, cotton, wool, etc. At first provide significant contrast for the child—introduce something very rough and then something very smooth. As the child becomes able to tolerate that stimulation, introduce textures which are not so obviously contrasting.

Tactile Activities

#34

Sandwich or Tostado

Play "sandwich" or "tostado." Ask a child to lie on a mat or comforter and to "be" the bread. Then ask another child to be a favorite "filling" and to lie on the bread. For example, the child can pretend to be "ham," another can pretend to be "cheese." Then use bean bags, koosch balls, or pillows to be the extras—pickles, jalapeno peppers, etc.

Tactile Activities
#35
Pyramid

Ask two children to lie face down on a mat. Then help another child lie on top of the other two, placed as if stacking logs. As the children get more comfortable, increase the base to three, four, or five children and build each level above with one less child.

Tactile Activities
#36
Water Play

Particularly in the hot summer and early fall, encourage the children to engage in water play. Have the children in swimsuits or play shorts. The children can then be free to play:

Sponge "Fights"

Let the children throw water-soaked sponges at each other. Set limits—the sponges should not be thrown at the face.

Tactile Activities
#37
Sprinkler/Hose (Water Play)

Allow the children to move in any way under a sprinkler or through water coming out of a hose.

Tactile Activities
#38
"Slip and Slide" (Water Play)

Build your own "slip and slide" (available commercially) by putting water from a hose on large sheets of plastic. Let the children crawl, creep, or knee-walk on the plastic. Avoid walking/running because it is very slippery.

Tactile Activities
#39
Texture Play

Allow the child to play in a box filled with sand, mud, styrofoam pellets, popcorn (popped and unpopped), oatmeal, uncooked beans, uncooked rice, puffed rice, mashed potatoes. Ask the child to find an object submerged in the "box."

Tactile Activities
#40
Body Painting

Ask one child to paint a partner's body part with shaving cream, whipped cream or pudding. For example, "Michael, paint Ernesto's foot with shaving cream." "Theresa, paint CArlos' face with chocolate pudding." This is also an outstanding body image activity.

Tactile Activities
#41
Roll-em-Ups

Roll the child into a sheet, blanket, carpet, towel or mat. Encourage the child to try to get out. Initially, wrap the child loosely and leave one arm or one leg free. Eventually, wrap the child more tightly.

Tactile Activities
#42
Cover-em-Ups

Cover the child with a large parachute, blanket, or sheet. Encourage the child to get out from under the cover. Initially, allow the child to be near an edge of the cover and, if necessary, have an arm or leg exposed.

Tactile Activities
#43
Mummy Making

Have the children work in pairs. Ask one child to be the "mummy" and his/her partner to be the "mummy maker." Ask the mummy to assume a position and hold it while the mummy maker wraps the mummy in toilet paper. The goal is to wrap the mummy so that only his/her eyes and mouth have slits. If possible, take a Polaroid snapshot of the mummy before s/he breaks out of the wrapping and comes back to life. This is also an excellent body image activity.

Tactile Activities
#44
Draw a Shape

Draw a shape on the child's back, forehead, arms, legs, or hands. Ask the child to identify the shape without "peeking." If working with the child on numbers or letters, these can be drawn on the child's body as well.

Proprioceptive Activities
#45
Rhythmic Activities

Ask the child to bend, stretch, twist, or curl specific body parts. The songs on the Body Image/Body Part Identification tape are particularly good:

What a Miracle
Walter the Waltzing Worm
Flick a Fly
Swing, Shake, Twist
Bean Bag
Bean Bag Boogie I and II
Hokey, Pokey
On the Count of Five

Proprioceptive Activities
#46
Push, Pull, and Carry

Ask the child to be involved in push, pull, and carrying activities. The child should push, pull, and carry objects of different weights, different shapes, different sizes, and using different patterns. For example, ask, the child to:

pull/push a partner on a scooter
pull/push one child, then another, and tell which is heavier
carry a heavy bag of groceries and a light bag and tell which is heavier

Proprioceptive Activities
#47
Arm and Leg Wrestle

Have two children arm wrestle. Facing each other, ask the children to grasp right to right or left to left hands, keeping elbows on a desk/table. Each child tries to push the other's hand down to the desk.

Have two children leg wrestle. Lying supine, hip to hip, ask the child to intertwine legs and try to pull the other over.

Proprioceptive Activities
#48
Simon Says

Ask the children to play "Simon Says," focusing on a variety of body positions. For example,

Simon says, "Touch your ear."
Simon says, "Touch your nose."
Simon says, "Touch your toes."
Simon says, "Touch your knees."
"Touch your head."

Proprioceptive Activities
#49
Move Through it All

Ask the children to move (crawl, creep, walk, roll in chair) on and through:

grass
sand
mud
tall grass
water

Proprioceptive Activities
#50
Stationary Statue Maker

Have the teacher or another child be the "statue maker." The statue maker should carefully place the child's body and limbs in a given position. The statue can be as complex or as simple as needed for each given child. Have the statue hold the position. Then "shake out" the statue and ask the child to put him/herself back into the "statue" position.

Proprioceptive Activities
#51
Follow the Jump Rope

Place a jump rope on the floor. Ask the child to lie down following the path of the rope.

Proprioceptive Activities
#52
Be My Twin

Put a "gumby" or a rag doll into a given position on the floor. Ask the child to duplicate the given body position.

Proprioceptive Activities
#53
Stick Figure Children

Draw a stick figure on butcher paper or on the blackboard. Ask the children to assume the same position. The body positions can be as complex or as simple as necessary for the children within the class.

Proprioceptive Activities
#54
Angels in the Snow

Ask the child to lie down on his/her back on brown butcher paper. Holding crayons in both hands, ask the child to move his/her arms up and down, maintaining contact with the paper throughout.

This can be particularly fun at Christmas, as you can then make individual "angels" by finishing the drawing.

Auditory Activities
#55
Make a Different Noise

Ask the children to take turns making music with a variety of instruments, bought and homemade. Then ask each child to use one particular instrument and follow the beat of a march.

Auditory Activities
#56
Pick the Right Instrument

Have two musical instruments in front of a child. Ask the child to close his/her eyes. Make music with one of the instruments. Ask the child to choose the instrument which was just used.

Auditory Activities
#57
Pick a Voice

Use a tape recorder to record each child speaking. Let the class listen to one tape, identifying the fact that it is the voice of one of two children. Ask the children in the class to identify which child is speaking. As the group becomes better at identifying the children's voices, have the class listen to a tape, selecting the child's voice from several/many.

Auditory Activities
#58
Animal Sounds

Have the children listen to a tape or song which includes animal sounds. Ask the children to try to duplicate the sounds.

Auditory Activities
#59
Find Your Friends

Assign each child in the room to make one of two particular noises or sounds. For example, ask three children to be "donkeys" and three children to be "cows." Ask the children to make the sounds throughout the process of finding every other child in the room also assigned to be a donkey or cow.

Auditory Activities
#60
Follow the Voice

Have the child crawl, creep, or walk around the room with her eyes closed, following the teacher's voice.

Auditory Activities
#61
Beep Ball Catch

Ask two children to sit facing one another, with eyes closed. Ask the children to roll a beep ball back and forth to each other.

Auditory Activities
#62
Follow the Beat

Ask one child to clap or stamp in a beat/pattern of his choice. Ask the other children to try to duplicate the beat/pattern.

This activity is particularly valuable for group activities in which one of the children is more physically involved than others. That child can be the "leader."

Auditory Activities
#63
Follow My Music

Give each child a musical instrument—cymbals, tambourine, lemme sticks, drum, etc. Ask one child to create a beat/pattern with the instrument and ask the others to follow the beat/pattern.

This activity is particularly valuable for group activities in which one of the children is more physically involved than others. This child can experience the thrill of being the leader.

Auditory Activities
#64
Follow the Bouncing Ball

Throw a ball into the air and ask the children to shake/hit/strike his/her musical instrument every time the ball hits the floor.

Visual Activities
#65
Follow the Balloon

Ask the children to follow the flight of a balloon with their eyes. This is more effective if you ask the children to follow the balloon by pointing at it with a finger.

Visual Activities
#66
Follow the Bouncing Ball

Ask the child to follow the flight of a bouncing ball. At first, allow the child to move his/her head, if necessary. Eventually, ask the child to hold the head still, moving only the eyes to track the flight of the ball.

Use different balls. Vary the type to vary the type of bounce. Use a highly inflated ball, an underinflated ball, a nerf ball, or a punch ball.

Visual Activities
#67
Blowing Bubbles

Ask the child to blow bubbles and then break the bubbles with a pointed finger. You can ask the child to work with a partner—one blows the bubbles and one breaks them.

Visual Activities
#68
<u>Red Light, Green Light</u>

Play "red light, green light" with two flashlights covered with red or green cellophane. The teacher or a designated student stands in front of the group. The leader holds two flashlights—one red = stop and one green = go. The leader then flashes alternately the two colors. Students can move forward, trying to reach the leader, only when the green light is shining; students must "freeze" when the light is red.

Visual Activities
#69
<u>Follow the Flashlight</u>

Darken the room. Ask a child to follow the circle of light created by a flashlight on the floor. This activity can be individualized for each student. For example, a student who can only crawl a short distance can try to put one body part into the circle of light. A "good mover" can be asked to jump from place to place to follow the circle of light.

BODY IMAGE
#70
Identify Primary Parts

Ask the child to identify his/her own primary body parts by touching them. Then ask the child to identify primary body parts on a picture or painting of a person.

Body Image
#71
Identify Body Parts on a Partner

Ask the child to identify primary body parts on a partner. For example, "Ike, touch Jimmy's back" or "Shamike, touch Deidra's head."

Body Image
#72
Identify Secondary Body Parts

Repeat #70 and #71 with secondary body parts.

Body Image
#73
Sock Walk

Have the child put his/her hands into clean socks. Draw shoes on the socks and explain to the child that his/her hands will now "walk," "run," "tiptoe" or "dance" on the body part named. For example,

"walk on your legs"
"tiptoe on your stomach"
"dance on your head"

Body Image
#74
My Senses

Read the poem "My senses" as the child does the action described below:

My eyes are for seeingPoint to eyes
I can see with my eyes.Look around.
My ears are for hearing.Point to ears.
I can hear with my ears.Cup ear.
My nose is for smelling.Point to nose.
I can smell with my nose.Sniff the air.
My tongue is for tasting.Point to tongue.
I can taste with my tongue.Pretend to lap.
My fingers are for touching.Wiggle fingers.
I can touch with my fingers.Touch something.

Body Image
#75
Gumby

Place a "Gumby" doll in a given position. Then ask the child to duplicate Gumby's position. You can do the same thing with a Raggedy Ann, Raggedy Andy, or other type of cloth doll.

Body Image
#76
Angels in the Snow

Ask the child to perform "Angels in the Snow," lying flat on back, and then flat on stomach. Fist, have the child move homologously, arms and legs move together. Second, have the child move homolaterally, arms and legs on one side of the body move together. Third, have the child move contralaterally—left arm moves with right leg, and right arms moves with left leg. If possible, do this in the sand so child can see the result.

Body Image
#77
Relate to Other Objects

Give the child an opportunity to relate his known body parts to other objects. For example, "Can you lie on your tummy on the floor?" "Can you put your back on the wall?" "Can you put your bottom into the hula hoop?"

Body Image
#78
Move in Patterns

Ask if the child can move his/her body in a particular pattern. For example,

"Can you crawl on this Figure 8?"
"Can you creep on this circle?"
"Can you walk on this triangle?"
"Can you walk backward around this stop sign?"
"Can you run on this rectangle?
"Can you run backwards on this 'NO' sign?"

Body Image
#79
Relate to 3-D Objects

Give the child the opportunity to explore the relationship between his/her body and large, open 3-D objects. For example:

"Can you climb into that box?"
"Can you fit into this smaller box?"
"Can you climb under the chair?"

Body Image
#80
Make a Shape

Ask the child/children to create "shapes" with his/her body. For example:

"Can you make your body look like a circle?"
"Can you and three friends make a triangle with your bodies?"
"Can you and a partner make a rectangle with your body?"

Body Image
#81
Move in a Smaller Space

Let the children explore their bodies in slowly decreasing space. For example, ask the children to creep within a given area without touching anyone or anything. Slowly decrease the amount of space in which they move.

The major rule in this activity is that the children may not touch anyone else while moving.

Body Image
#82
Simon Says

The teacher should assume the role of "Simon." Ask the child to do activities, at their own level, which require them to identify their body parts. For example,

"Simon says, touch your nose."
"Simon says, touch your toes."
"Simon says, touch your right ear with your left hand."
"Simon says, touch your nose with the little finger on your left hand."

Body Image
#83
Twister

Play the commercial game "Twister" or make your own Twister game on a felt-backed vinyl tablecloth, or draw with chalk on a sidewalk. The child is asked to put a hand on a red dot, or put a foot on a blue square, etc. You can make this as complex or as simple as you would like. This can also be done to teach other concepts. For example, the child can be asked to put a hand on a given safety sign, a letter, or number.

Body Image
#84
Own Body Puzzle

Make "butcher paper" tracings of each child's body. Then make "my own body" puzzles for each child by laminating and then cutting up the traced body.

The child can have an initial puzzle that is only the top half and lower half of the body. Then, as the child begins to acquire body image, the child's puzzle can include arms, legs, and head.

Body Image
#85
Sugar Shadow

Make "powdered sugar" tracings of the child. Ask the child to lie on the floor and shake powdered sugar from a small canister around the child's frame. Then help the child get up without disturbing the shadow.

Body Image
#86
<u>Hello, My Name is Joe</u>

Have children say the following poem with the teacher. Repeat it with a definite rhythm:

Hello, my name is Joe. I have a wife and three kids. And I work in a button factor.

My boss came up to me and said, "You busy?" I said "No." He said, "Good," then push the button with your good hand. **(Note: You can add as many body parts as you would like, as the children learn the poem.)** Then finish with the last verse:

My boss came up to me and said, "You busy?" I said, "YES. I QUIT!"

Body Image
#87
<u>Rhythmic Activities</u>

The following songs/dances are really effective in developing body image in "rug rats:"

<u>Sally the Swinging Snake</u>
Sally the Swinging Snake
On the Count of Five
<u>Walter the Walzing Worm</u>
What a Miracle
Walter the Waltzing Worm
Flick a Fly
Swing, Shake, Twist
<u>Kids in Motion</u>
Bean Bag Boogie I & II
<u>Get a Good Start</u>
Warm-up Time

LOCOMOTOR PATTERNS

General Introduction

The goal of gross motor programming is for the child to "own" a variety of locomotor skills. "Ownership" means that the child can perform a locomotor skill automatically and without thought. In order to "own" a particular locomotor skill, the child must have the opportunity to use the skill in a variety of situations. This can be done by manipulating the variables of movement: time, space, force and flow.

For example, the walk can be modified:

Time:

Walk fast. Walk to the beat of a drum.

Space:

Walk around the chair. Walk on the line.
Walk holding a partner's hand.

Force:

Walk like a giant—stomp.
Walk like a ballet dancer—on tiptoes.

Flow:

Walk 3 steps—Stop—Walk 3 steps—Stop

Roll
#88

Time

Ask the child to:

Roll fast.
Roll slow.
Roll, increasing speed.
Go on a "rolling Ride."

Ask the child to lie down on the edge of a sheet or blanket on a mat. Roll the child in the sheet/blanket. When the child is wrapped up, grab the edge of the sheet and lift so child rolls quickly out of the sheet/blanket.

Roll
#89
<u>Space</u>

Ask the child to:

Roll with arms at sides of body.
Roll with arms above the head.
Roll up and down an incline.
Roll on a variety of surfaces—mat, carpet, grass.
Roll with a partner.

Partners should face each other and wrap arms around each other. Holding on tightly, roll together.

Roll
#90
<u>Force</u>

Ask the child to:

Roll hard.
Roll gently.
Roll in a carpeted barrel.
Do a rocking roller.

Have the child to lie in the middle of a sheet or blanket. Teacher and other children hold the edges of two ends of the sheet. Alternately, lift the sheet edge so the child rolls towards children at other end of sheet; then they should reciprocate by lifting so the child rolls back and forth.

Roll
#91
Flow

Ask the child to:
Roll in one direction; stop; roll in the other direction.
Roll; stop; roll; stop.
Do a rolling ride—
Roll the child into a sheet, blanket, carpet, towel or mat. Let them try to get out.
Do different types of rolls—
Log roll, segmental roll, egg roll, shoulder roll, forward and backward rolls.

Crawl
#92
Time

Ask the child to:
Crawl slow, then fast.
Ask the child to crawl and stop.
The following songs are excellent:
Song about Slow/Fast
The Freeze

Crawl
#93
Space

Ask the child to:
Crawl to a favorite doll/toy.
Crawl through a tunnel (chairs and old sheets).
Crawl through an obstacle course (over, under, around, and
through objects).
Crawl under classmate's spread legs.
Crawl backwards.

Crawl
#94
Force

Ask the child to:
Crawl pushing a ball with his/her nose.
Crawl with a partner riding on his/her back.
Crawl with small weights attached to wrists/ankles.

Crawl
#95
Flow

Ask the child to:
Crawl up an incline; stop; turn around; crawl down.

Creep
#96
Time

Ask the child to:
Crawl to fast music.
Crawl to slow music.

Creep
#97
Space

Ask the child to:
Creep forward, holding a bean bag on the head.
Creep over classmates lying face down in a series.
Creep through a series of desks.

Creep
#98
Force

Ask the child to:
Creep through sand, mud, tall grass, etc.
Creep while pulling a classmate on a scooter.

Creep
#99
<u>Flow</u>

Ask the child to:

Creep forward 10 feet; stop; creep backward 10 feet.

Walk/Run
#100
<u>Time</u>

Ask the child to:

March to one of the following songs:

Consider Yourself	*Preschool Aerobic Fun*
Marching Along	*Preschool Aerobic Fun*

Vary the pace/tone of the walk. Ask the child to do a "happy" walk or a "sad" walk.

Walk/run to the beat of a drum, a shake of a tambourine, or a hand clap.

Walk/Run
#101
<u>Space</u>

Ask the child to:

Walk/run keeping feet on a line at least as wide as the child's shoulder. As the child becomes more proficient, gradually narrow the width of the line.

Walk/run on a pattern on the floor—square, circle, etc.

Walk/run on a more complex pattern—zig-zag and figure 8 patterns.

Walk/run through a series of cones.

Walk/Run
#102
Space

Ask the child to:

Walk/run over a series of parallel lines, 12 to 18 inches apart, without touching a line.

Walk/run over a series of parallel suspended strings. Begin with a string 1 inch above the floor and gradually raise the strings until the string is at the child's knee level.

Walk the length of the ladder, on the floor, without touching the rungs.

Walk the length of the ladder touching only the rungs.

Walk/Run
#103
Space

Ask the child to:

Walk/run with his/her hands placed on specific body parts.

For example, "Can you walk with your hands on our head?"

Walk/run on his/her tiptoes.

Walk/run on his/her heels.

Soldier walk.

Walk/Run
#104
Space

Ask the child to:

Walk/run while moving through different levels. For example,

"Be as tall as you can be while you walk/run."

"Be as 'fat' as you can be while you walk run."

Walk/Run
#105
Force

Ask the child to:

Walk/run on different surfaces—grass, cement, linoleum, "wet" linoleum, sand...

Walk/run, holding objects of different weights in each hand.

Walk/Run
#106
Flow

Ask the child to

Walk like Dorothy, the Tin Man, the Lion, and the Scarecrow, after reading the *Wizard of Oz*.

Walk/run forward, turn 180 degrees, walk backward.

Walk/run backward, turn 360 degrees, walk backward.

Walk/run forward. Stop and touch toes. Walk forward.

Walk/Run
#107
Flow

Ask the child to run, using the following music:

Simon Says Jog Along	*Get a Good Start*
Song about Slow/Fast	*Walter the Waltzing Worm*
Chug a Long Choo Choo	*Preschool Aerobic Fun*
Run Run Run in Place	*Preschool Aerobic Fun*

Jump/Hop
#108
Time

Ask the child to:

Jump/hop to a drum beat or hand clap.

Jump/hop to music with a 2/2 or 4/4 beat.

Jump/hop following the bouncing of a ball.

Jump/Hop
#109
Space
Ask the child to:
Step down from a stable object 1" off floor.
Step down from a stable object 3" off floor.
Jump down from a stable object 1" off floor.
Jump down from a stable object 3" off floor.
Jump down from a stable object 6" off floor.
Jump down from a stable object 12" off floor.

Jump/Hop
#110
Space
Ask the child to:
Jump/hop over a line on the floor.
Jump/hop over and back, across a line on the floor, forward/backward.
Jump/hop over and back, across a line on the floor, side/side.
Play "sizzling snake." Make a jump rope slither on the floor and have the children jump to avoid being "bitten."

Jump/Hop
#111
Space
Ask the child to:
Jump/hop reaching to touch a suspended balloon.
Jump/hop reaching to touch a suspended balloon, in a series.

Jump/Hop
#112
Force

Ask the child to:
Play "Kangaroo." The child assumes an erect body position with flexion only at knees and ankles. S/he springs to complete extension and then flexes to land.

Jump/Hop
#113
Force

Ask the child to:
Play leaping frog. The child assumes a semi-squat position and springs forward to another semi-squat position. Do not allow the child to move into a position of full flexion at the knee. Make "Ribbid" sounds while you recite the poem "Freddy the Frog."

Freddy the frog,
Jumped in the bog,
Jump, Freddy, jump.
He sang all day.
He jumped and played,
Jump, Freddy, jump.

Jump/Hop
#114
Force

Have the children jump over an object on the floor, while you and the children recite:

Jack be nimble,
Jack be quick,
Jack, jump over the candle stick.
Jack, jump high.
Jack, jump low.
Jack, jump over or burn your toe.

Jump/Hop
#115
<u>Force</u>

Ask the child to jump while you recite the poem:

Have you seen my jumping bean?
Strangest thing I've ever seen.
It jumped over my plate and onto the floor,
Before I knew it, it jumped out the door.
Jump, jumping bean, jump.

Jump/Hop
#116
<u>Force</u>

Ask the children to hop while you recite "Peter Cottontail."

Here comes Peter Cottontail,
Hopping down the bunny trail,
Hippity, Hoppity,
Spring is on its way.

Jump/Hop
#117
<u>Flow</u>

Ask the child to jump forward, backward, and sideward, while reciting the following poem:

Have you seen the jumping bean?
Strangest thing I've ever seen.
It jumped off my plate and onto the floor,
Before I knew it, it jumped out the door.
Jump, jumping bean, jump.

Wheelchair Roll
#118
Time

Ask the child to:

Roll the chair to the beat of a drum or tambourine, or a hand clap.

Roll, varying pace, using songs like "Song about Slow/Fast," or "Freeze."

Wheelchair Roll
#119
Space

Ask the child to:

Roll between two lines.

Roll, keeping body centered, over lines forming shapes or patterns—circles, squares, figure 8s, etc.

Roll around between and through cones, classmates, chairs, desks, etc.

Wheelchair Roll
#120
Space

Ask the child to:

Roll on a variety of surfaces—grass, carpet, sand, cement, linoleum, tile, etc.

Roll up and down inclines.

Roll over door jams, sticks, small stones, etc.

Roll backwards, eventually repeating above activities.

Wheelchair Roll
#121
<u>Force</u>

Ask the child to:

Use one "max" roll to travel as far as possible with one roll.

Use two "max" rolls to travel as far as possible with two rolls.

Roll pulling a classmate on a scooterboard.

Roll with a classmate on his/her lap.

Wheelchair Roll
#122
<u>Flow</u>

Ask the child to:

Roll forward 3 strokes, stop, roll backward 3 strokes.

Roll forward, pivot 180 degrees, roll forward.

Roll backward, pivot 360 degrees, roll backward.

Wheelchair Roll
#123
<u>Flow</u>

Ask the child to:

Complete an obstacle course which includes moving through cones, over 2 x 2s, up and down ramps.

CROSS-LATERAL INTEGRATION

Cross-Lateral Integration
#124
Mixed-Up Creeper

Place a rope on a mat or on a carpeted floor. Ask the child to creep while moving forward. As the child, his/her right hand should be placed on the left side of the rope; as the child moves, his/her left hand should be placed on the right side of the rope. The child literally is creeping while crossing hands over the rope.

Cross-Lateral Integration
#125
17 Pick-Up

Scatter 17 blocks, large marbles, dominoes, or small plastic dinosaurs on the right side of the child's body. Holding the child's head still, ask the child to pick up the objects with the right hand and place them, one at a time, in a can placed on the left side of the child's body. Repeat, having the child move the objects with the left hand.

NOTE: The size of the objects should be determined by the child's fine-motor coordination skills. In order to focus on cross-lateral integration, the child should move objects s/he can control with ease.

Cross-Lateral Integration
#126
Crossing the River

Ask a child to lie supine on a scooter and pull self hand-over-hand along a heavy rope (tug-of-war type) suspended 18"-24" above the child's body. The child should move head first, pretending that s/he is crossing a river. Preferably, the river is full of crocodiles, or alligators, or anything else that makes the activity fun

Cross-Lateral Integration
#127
Crossing the Desert

Ask a child to lie prone on a scooter and pull self hand-over-hand along a heavy rope (tug-of-war type) suspended 6"-12" above the child's body. The child should move head first, pretending that s/he is struggling through the desert, hoping to find water.

Cross-Lateral Integration
#128
Crazy Cross-over

Place a straight tape line on the floor. Put red objects on the left side of the line and blue objects on the right side. Ask the child to crawl or creep along the line. As s/he moves along, the child should pick up the red objects with the left hand and lace them over the line, on the right side of the line. The child should pick up the blue objects with the right hand and transfer them to the left side of the body.

NOTE: The child should only move one object at a time and should keep shoulders perpendicular to the line of travel.

Cross-Lateral Integration
#129
Pat-a-Cake

Simply play "pat-a-cake." It is a great activity to develop cross-lateral integration.

Cross-Lateral Integration
#130
"Pillow-a-Way"

The teacher and the child should sit, kneel, or stand facing each other. They should join hands with arms crossed in front. Ask another child to place a pillow on top of the crossed arms. The teacher and the child should try to keep the pillow on the arms while swinging the arms back and forth, up as high as possible.

Cross-Lateral Integration
#131
Vibrator Vibes

Put a vibrator in the child's right hand. Call out body parts and ask the child to "vibrate" that part on the left side of the body, the left elbow, the left knee, the left thigh, the left ankle, etc.

Make sure the child does not turn the shoulders while crossing the midline of the body.

Repeat, using the child's left hand.

Cross-Lateral Integration
#132
Twist-Over

Place a rope or low balance beam on the floor. Ask the child to walk with a "scissors" gait—the right foot is placed on the left side of the rope/beam and the left foot is placed on the right side of the rope/beam.

Cross-Lateral Integration
#133
Mirror-Mirror

Ask the child to mirror the teacher's movement. Move specifically so that the child will need to cross the midline of the body, i.e., touch right hand to left shoulder, left hand to right foot, etc.

Cross-Lateral Integration
#134
Ninja-Turtle

Ask the child to hand from a horizontal bar or stall bar. Ask the child to kick his/her left leg up and across midline to kick a pillow (monster, "bad guy," etc.) held in front of the right side of the child's body.

Repeat asking the child to kick the right leg up and across the midline to pick something on the left side of the child's body.

Cross-Lateral Integration
#135
Crazy Kicker

Ask a child to sit, with back to wall. Roll a ball to the right side of the child's body, and ask the child to pick the ball with the left foot.

Repeat, with the other foot.

Make sure that the child keeps his/her back square against the wall.

Cross-Lateral Integration
#136
Stack-a-Block

Place an assortment of blocks on the right side of the body. Ask the child to pick up one block at a time and make a stack of blocks on the left side of his/her body. Repeat, asking the child to move blocks from left side of body, with left hand, and place blocks in a stack on the right side of body.

Make sure that the child does not turn the shoulders while stacking the blocks.

Cross-Lateral Integration
#137
Crazy Spinner

Ask the child to lie prone on a scooter and spin self by alternately crossing hands. Ask the child to spin clockwise and then counter-clockwise.

FITNESS
Sitting Aerobicizes
Warm-up Activity
#138
Shoulder Shrugs

Ask the child to shrug both shoulders simultaneously. The cue, "Try to touch your shoulders to your ears" works well.

Sitting Aerobicizes
Warm-up Activity
#139
Shoulder Circles

Ask the child to roll his/her shoulders forward. Then have the child roll shoulders backward.

Sitting Aerobicizes
Transition Activity
#140
"Big" Hand Claps

Ask the children to clap his/her hands. At first, the child should clap regularly. Gradually, the child should begin making the clapping motion bigger and bigger. Eventually all muscles of the arms and shoulder girdle should be involved.

Sitting Aerobicizes
Transition Activity
#141
Clap Thighs - Clap Hands

Take both hands and slap thighs. Then clap hands together. Repeat this motion, gradually making the motion bigger.

Sitting Aerobicizes
Aerobic Activity
#142
Simultaneous "Above the Head" Punches

Child reaches both hands toward the sky at the same time, holding hands in a fist. Allow hands to return to lap to recover. Repeat the motion.

Sitting Aerobicizes
Aerobic Activity
#143
Simultaneous "In Front of Chest" Punches

Child "punches" the air in front of his/her chest by moving arms from flexion to extension, holding hands in a fist. Return hands to lap to recover. Vary activity by having child open and extend fingers during the "punch."

Sitting Aerobicizes
Aerobic Activity
#144
Simultaneous "To the Sides" Punches

Child "punches" the air, moving both arms from flexion to extension at shoulder level to the sides. Relax by returning hands to lap. Repeat.

Sitting Aerobicizes
Aerobic Activity
#145
Alternating Punches

Perform any of the above punches—above the head, in front of chest, and to the sides—but alternate arm action. One arm should be in extension while the other is in flexion.

Sitting Aerobicizes
Aerobic Activity
#146
Hands on Hips Twist

Ask child to put hands on hips and twist trunk to right and then left while sitting in an erect posture.

Sitting Aerobicizes
Aerobic Activity
#147
Arms at Sides Trunk Twist

Ask child to hold arms extended to sides, at shoulder level. Alternately twist trunk to right and then left, while sitting in an erect posture.

Sitting Aerobicizes
Aerobic Activity
#148
Cross in Front

Ask child to hold arms out to sides, at shoulder level. Keeping arms straight throughout, draw arms toward and then pat midline of the body. Alternate which arm is "on top;" first the right, then the left.

Sitting Aerobicizes
Aerobic Activity
#149
Cross Over Head

Ask child to hold arms above head. Keeping arms straight throughout, move one arm in front of head, one in back. Note: This activity involves a great deal of shoulder rotation.

Sitting Aerobicizes
Aerobic Activity
#150

Simultaneous Arm Pumping

Ask the child to hold both arms with elbows bent so that there is a ninety degree angle at elbow.

Pump arms forward and backward simultaneously.

Sitting Aerobicizes
Aerobic Activity
#151

Alternate Arm Pumping

Ask the child to hold both arms with elbows bent so that there is a ninety degree angle at elbow. Pump arms forward and backward alternately, using the same motion that is used in running.

Sitting Aerobicizes
Aerobic Activity
#152

Both Hands Toe Touches

Ask the child to sit erect in chair. Then ask the child to bend down to touch both toes and ten return to fully erect position.

Sitting Aerobicizes
Aerobic Activity
#153

Alternate Hands Toe Touches

Ask the child to sit erect in chair. Then ask the child to bend to touch right hand to left foot, left hand to right foot. Return to erect position between each toe touch.

Sitting Aerobicizes
Aerobic Activity
#154

Arm Circles

Ask the child to sit erect in the chair. Holding both arms straight out to the sides, the child should start by making small circles and build to making huge arm circles.

ANIMAL ACTIONS

These animal actions can be used to accompany a story that you create or read from a book. These actions can also accompany a unit or class day devoted to "Going to the Farm," "Off to the Circus" or "Pets on Parade." These are best taught if the child has had an opportunity to see the animal—in a picture, a video, or "in person."

Animal Actions
#155
Peeking Turtle

The child lies prone, chin tucked to neck, with head covered by a "shell" (blanket, small mat, big bean bag) and then peeks out from under the mat or blanket, by lifting head. Reverse action, then, by having the child pretend s/he saw something scary, and tucking head to return to position "in shell."

Animal Actions
#156
Stretching Kitty

The child lies tucked up in a ball on his/her side, pretending to be asleep. Then the child stretches all four paws, first independently and then simultaneously, until awake.

Animal Actions
#157
Crazy Snake

The child pretends to be a snake who can't move forward. The child rolls over and over and over...first in one direction then another. The "crazy" snake ultimately ends up in the same place.

Animal Actions
#158
<u>Sneaky Alligator</u>

The child moves in a prone position, with body completely in contact with the floor. The child pulls his body along with his arms, leaving his "tail" to drag along the floor. A child who is unable to do this may be able to do it if placed prone on a long scooter. The less strength the child has, the longer the scooter should be.

Animal Actions
#159
<u>Clapping Seal</u>

The child pulls his lower body along the floor, while supporting his/her body in a push-up position. Occasional stops to rock and "clap fins" make this a great deal more fun. If the child is unable to support self in this position, the child's chest could be supported by a bolster or pillow.

Animal Actions
#160
<u>Hopping Bunny</u>

The child assumes a hands and knees position (with lower leg in contact with the floor). The child moves both hands forward together and pulls (slides) legs up towards the hands. Then the child moves hands forward and repeats activity (homologous movement).

Animal Actions
#161
<u>Angry Cat</u>

The child assumes an all-fours position on the floor. Then, hissing loudly, the child presses his/her back up into an arch. The child holds the position for several seconds, while hissing, and then the child relaxes.

Animal Actions
#162
Grazing Cow

Ask the child to move on all-fours, while pushing a bean bag with his/her nose along the floor. The child should pretend to stop, every once in a while, and "chew his cud."

Animal Actions
#163
Bucking Horse

Ask the child to assume an all-fours position on a mat or quilt. Put bean bags flat on the child's back and ask the child to "buck" to throw the bean bags off his/her back.

Animal Actions
#164
Silly Dog

The child moves on all-fours, using opposite sides of the body alternately. The child moves right hand and right knee forward together and then left hand and left leg forward together (homolateral movement).

Animal Actions
#165
Smart Dog

The child moves on all-fours, contralaterally.The child moves the right hand and left knee forward together; then the child moves the left hand and the right knee forward together (contralateral movement).

Animal Actions
#166
Puppy with a Sore Paw

The child starts on all-fours and then moves using both hands and one foot or one hand and both feet. Encourage the child to experiment with redistribution of weight necessary to make movement adjustments. Encourage the child to move in all directions.

Animal Actions
#167
Dizzy Dog

The child moves in an all-fours walk, but moves with arms crossed in front of his/her body. Have the child experiment with use of each arm as "lead."

Animal Actions
#168
Creepy Crab

The child supports his/her body on both hands and feet with buttocks facing the floor. Ask the child to experiment with moving forward, backward, and sideward. If the child is unable to support his/her body off the floor, the child could sit on a scooter, or "scoot" on the floor with his/her buttocks on the floor.

Animal Actions
#169
Peanut-Eating Elephant

The child walks, bent from waist, holding arms together in front of body, swing "trunk" from side to side. Occasionally, ask child to reach down and pick up "peanut" from floor (beanbag, yarn ball, or real peanut).

Animal Actions
#170
Jumping Kangaroo

The child assumes an erect body position with flexion only at knees and ankles. S/he springs to complete extension and then flexes to land.

Make it more fun by asking the child to jump, with a backpack or "fanny" pack about stomach, carrying something in the pouch.

Animal Actions
#171
Leaping Frog

The child assumes a semi-squat position and springs forward to another semi-squat position. Do not allow the child to move into a position of full flexion at the knee.

Animal Actions
#172
"Inching" Inch Worm

The child assumes a long push-up position and then slowly edges his/her feet up to meet the hands while the hands stay in the same position. (The child will be in a classic toe-touch position.) Then the child edges his hands forward to return to the push-up position while feet remain stationary.

Animal Actions
#173
Kicking Mule

The child places his/her hands on the floor and gently kicks his/her legs into the air, supporting his/her body weight on the hands.

Animal Actions
#174
Lumbering Bear

The child moves on hands and feet in a homolateral pattern. The child simultaneously moves the right hand and right foot forward and then the left hand and left foot. The child tries to "lumber" from one side to another.

Animal Actions
#175
Funky Penguin

Ask the child to stand with arms held tightly at sides of body and "waddle" from side to side. This can be a group activity if the children are asked to waddle in synchrony.

RELAXATION
#176
Basic Position

A child can practice basic relaxation techniques in a sitting or lying position. If relaxation is to be practiced sitting, the back should be straight, the head in alignment, and feet should be flat on the floor. Hands and arms should rest comfortably on the desk or the lap.

If lying, it is important that the child has the back flat on the floor with arms and legs rotated out away from the midline position. If the child is unable to lie on the floor with back flat, it may be necessary to put a pillow underneath the child's knees.

Relaxation
#177
Deep Breathing Exercise

Help the child be aware of her own breathing. Use techniques like asking the child to put her hand on her chest to feel the chest rise and fall. Ask the child to "slow down" his/her breathing. Repeat the process for at least five minutes.

Relaxation
#178
Head Circle

Ask the child to assume a sitting or standing position. Ask the child to slowly rotate his/her head in a full circle five times in one direction and five in the other.

Some children may prefer to keep their eyes open to prevent dizziness. It is usually easier to relax, however, with eyes closed.

Repeat for three to four minutes. Combine with controlled slow breathing.

Relaxation
#179
<u>Shoulder Rolls</u>

Ask the child to assume a sitting or standing position. Ask the child to slowly roll his/her shoulders in a complete circle, keeping the arms in a relatively vertical position. The child should roll his/her shoulders five times in one direction and then five in the other.

Combine with conscious slow-down of breathing.

Relaxation
#180
<u>Imagery Techniques</u>

Ask the child to pretend to be an ice cream cone melting in the hot sun. Combine this with deep breathing exercises.

Relaxation
#181
<u>Imagery Techniques</u>

Ask the child to pretend to be a sleepy puppy or kitty, curling up to go to sleep. Have the child alternate stretching and yawning.

Relaxation
#182
<u>Progressive Relaxation</u>

Ask the child to assume a sitting or back lying position. Ask the child to tighten his/her face, and relax. Using cues like asking the child to "crinkle" his/her or to make his/her face look like a "raisin" or a "prune."

Repeat the process for several minutes. Begin to ask questions to help the child to become more aware of the existence of tension in the body like, "Can you feel the difference?"

Combine with controlled, slow breathing.

Relaxation
#183
Progressive Relaxation

Ask the child to tighten the muscles in his/her arms. The best technique for eliciting this response is to ask the child to "make a fist" and squeeze. Alternate tightening and relaxing for several minutes.

Combine with controlled, slow breathing.

Relaxation
#184
Progressive Relaxation

Ask the child to tighten his/her stomach muscles and then relax. This is usually easiest if you put your hand on the child's stomach and ask the child to "suck it in."

Alternately contract and relax. Combine with controlled, slow breathing exercises.

Relaxation
#185
Progressive Relaxation

Ask the child to tighten the muscles in his upper legs. This usually works best if you ask the child to put his hands on his thigh and "make the leg hard."

Alternate the process of tightening and relaxing the muscle.

Combine with controlled, slow breathing.

Relaxation
#186
My Safest Place

Lead the children through a series of self-controlled "visions" to help the children picture the place, time, or setting that allows the children to relax. It is important not to create the scene, but rather to allow the child to create it. This is vital because what is relaxing to one child may be very frightening to another.

Use leading statements like,
"Picture the place where you feel safest."
"Picture the place where you most like to sleep."

Relaxation
#187
Relaxation Music

Ask the children to get into comfortable relaxation positions and then initiate controlled, slow breathing while listening to relaxation music like "Seagulls for Rest and Relaxation."

Cooperative Games
#188
Parachute Play - Peek and Wave

Ask the children to sit around a parachute (or a tie-dyed or colorful sheet) and grasp the edges. One child at a time crawls under the parachute into the center of the circle. Given a signal, the children on the outside of the circle lift the parachute and then drop one hand and wave at the child in the center. The child in the center waves back. Repeat 2 times for each child.

Cooperative Games
#189
Parachute Play - Popcorn

The children should sit or stand around the outside of the parachute. The teacher should place yarn balls or tennis balls on the parachute while children jiggle the parachute to make the balls bounce up and down.

Cooperative Games
#190
Parachute Play - Ripples and Waves

Ask the children to sit around the parachute and grasp it with both hands. Have the children move the parachute edge up and down 4 to 6 inches to cause "ripples." Alternate and have the children move the parachute 12 to 18 inches up and down to cause "waves."

Cooperative Games
#191
Parachute Play - Magic Mountain

Have the children grasp the edges/handles of the parachute. Make sure that the parachute is flat on the ground. On a given signal, the children should lift the parachute up over their heads to trap air and then, together, pull parachute to ground "trapping" the air, and holding the edges as if to seal the air in the mountain.

Cooperative Games
#192
Parachute Play - Trapped under the Magic Mountain

Repeat the activity explained in #191 but as the parachute is brought down to the ground, have the children move under parachute so when they create the seal to trap the air, all the children are caught under the magic mountain. If using a small parachute, one or two children can be trapped inside while the other children make the seal on the outside.

Cooperative Games
#193
Parachute Play - Find Your Spot

Have the children sit or stand and hold the parachute. One by one, each child should drop hold of the parachute and use one of the following locomotor patterns to go around the parachute and then retake original spot: wheelchair roll, walk, run, jump, gallop, or skip.

Cooperative Games
#194
Parachute Play - Spoke of the Wheel

Ask the child to grasp the parachute with one hand, each child using the same hand. Then the children, as a group, using the same locomotor pattern, move about the parachute center as if it is the parachute is a wheel.

Cooperative Games
#195
Wands and Ribbons

Each child has his/her own individual wand and ribbon. The intent is for each child in the group to be making the same pattern with the wand and ribbon at the same time. The patterns which are easy include: circles, vertical lines, horizontal lines, figure 8s, and small waves.

Cooperative Games
#196
"Don't Let it Touch the Ground"

Using a balloon, beachballs, or volleyballs, have a group of children try to keep the balloons or balls up in the air using any given body part—hands, head, etc. Initially, work in pairs or in small groups—as the students develop cooperative play skills, enlarge the group.

Cooperative Games
#197
Together now!

Ask the children to get into a line and perform the same locomotor activity. Children in wheelchairs can be involved by having a partner help, if needed, move the wheelchair. Ask the children to line up, hold each other by the waist and perform one of the following: walk forward, walk backward, run forward, run backward, and jump forward/backward.

Cooperative Games
#198
Earth Ball Pass

Ask the children to sit in a circle or in two lines facing each other. Using a huge playball or cage ball, ask the children to pass the ball back and forth and keep it in the air. At first, use the hands. Later, use the feet.

Cooperative Games
#199
Body Pass

Ask the children to lie down on their backs, close together like sardines in a can. Ask them to put their arms out straight and to "pass the body" of a friend from one end of the line to the other. The child being passed should lie on his/her back, rigid like a rod.

You will need to help them get started. Place stronger children next to children lacking strength. This is also an exceptional "touching" opportunity.

Cooperative Games
#200
Pinball Marching Marvel

Ask the children to stand in a circle with feet wide apart and touching. Then ask the children to lean over so their backsides are facing the center of the circle. Putting hands down, have them use them like pinball paddles to keep a large ball moving across and about the circle.

A child in a chair can simple use his/her arms as paddles at the sides of the chair. A child who needs to remain in a lying position can be one of the "bumpers."

Cooperative Games
#201
Partner Stand Up

Ask two children to sit with backs facing each other. Have them intertwine arms and then push simultaneously to a standing position.

This takes strength and coordination and may need to be practiced (a lot!). However, the beauty of it is that the children must work together to accomplish the goal.

Cooperative Games
#202
The Creature

The game begins as a simple game of tag. One child is designated as "it." When "it" tags a person, s/he joins hands and the "creature" gets larger and larger as each child is tagged. The children must hold hands as they try to encircle and tag each new child. When all children are part of the "creature," the game begins again.

Cooperative Games
#203
Forever Volleyball

Any number of children can play. Players can be seated or players can be standing. (It is wise for all children to assume the same position.) Any equal number of children should be on either side of a net suspended between the teams 2 feet above the average extended hand height. The intent of the game is to keep the beach ball or volleyball going back and forth over the net as many times as possible.

Cooperative Games
#204
Hug a Friend

Play a game of tag with the following simple modification. A child is "safe" if the child is hugging another child. Eventually, modify the rules so the only time a child is "safe" is if s/he is involved in a "group" hug with 3 or 4 children.

Cooperative Games
#205
Sardine Switch

have the children lie down on their stomachs, tightly squeezed together side-to-side. Have one child lie down at one end of the line of children and roll (no shoes or braces) across the "sardines" and take her new place at the other end, tightly squeezed next to the child who had been last.

Cooperative Games
#206
Sit With Me

One child sits with his/her legs apart in a V position on a chair. The child calls out the name of a child and says, for example, "Adam, come sit with me." Adam comes and sits down on the child's lap. Then Adam invites another child to sit on his lap and so on.

This can also be done sitting on the floor or in the grass.

Cooperative Games
#207
Hot Potato

The children are seated in a circle and can use hands or feet to pass an object—bean bag, nerf ball, large playground ball—about the circle as fast as possible to avoid getting "burned."

Cooperative Games
#208
Follow the Leader Over the Obstacle

One child is the leader. It is the leader's responsibility to choose a movement pattern everyone in the group can use to follow the leader over the obstacle.

Cooperative Games
#209
Let's Go Fly a Kite

Ask children to work in twos, threes, or fours to literally "fly a kite."

Cooperative Games
#210
Just One More

Identify one particular shape or object. Ask one child to get into the shape and continue to invite others until no more can fit (reminiscent of stuffing people into telephone booths or Volkswagen Beetles). For example, ask one child to stand with at least one foot in a hula hoop. Then, ask him/her to invite another, and another, and another, until no more can fit.

SUGGESTED MUSIC/SONGS

Easy Does It: Activity Songs for Basic Motor Skill Development. Freeport, NY: Educational Activities, Inc., Activity Records Inc., 1977.

Bean Bag
Circle Your Way
High Wire Artist

Greg & Steve. *Kidding Around with Greg and Steve*. Los Angeles: Youngheart Records, 1985

The Hugging Song
Believe in Yourself
Hokey Pokey (Part 1 and 2)

Greg & Steve. *We All Live Together, Volume 2*. Los Angeles: Youngheart Records, 1979.

Popcorn
The Freeze
Resting

Mod Marches. Freeport, NY: Educational Activities, Inc., Activity Records Inc., 1970.

Penny Lane
It's a Small World
Yellow Submarine

Palmer, Hap. *Creative Movement and Rhythmic Exploration.* Freeport, NY: Educational Activities, Inc., Activity Records Inc., 1971.

Moving Game - Part 1 and 2
Colored Ribbons
Teacher Who Couldn't Talk
Percussion Instruments

Palmer, Hap. *Pretend.* Freeport, NY: Educational Activities, Inc., Activity Records Inc., 1971.

The Friendly Giant
The Clown
Jumping Frog
Kite Song

Palmer, Hap. *Sally the Swinging Snake.* Freeport, NY: Educational Activities, Inc., Activity Records Inc., 1987.

Sally the Swinging Snake
On the Count of Five

Palmer, Hap. *Seagulls for Rest and Relaxation.* Freeport, NY: Educational Activities, Inc., Activity Records Inc., 1987.

All Selections

Palmer, Hap. *Walter the Waltzing Worm*. Freeport, NY: Educational Activities, Inc., Activity Records Inc., 1982.

What a Miracle
Walter the Waltzing Worm
Flick a Fly
Song About Slow, Song About Fast
Swing, Shake, Twist and Stretch
All the Ways of Jumping Up and Down

Stewart, Georgiana. *Bean Bag Activities & Coordination Skills*. Longbranch, NJ: KIMBO, 1989.

Who's Got the Bean Bag?
Bean Bag Rock
Pass the Bean Bag
Bean Bag Parade

Stewart, Georgiana. *Preschool Aerobic Fun*. Longbranch, NJ: KIMBO, 1989.

Wake-Up, Warm-Up
Hot Diggity
Movin' Every Day
Chug A Long Choo Choo
Run, Run, Run in Place
Consider Yourself
Marching Along Together

SUGGESTED REFERENCES

Cherry, C. *Creative Movement for the Developing Child: A Nursery School Handbook for Non-Musicians.* Belmont, CA: Lake Publishers, 1971.

Doray, M. *J is For Jump! Moving into Language Skills.* Belmont, CA: Lake Publishers, 1982.

Hillert, M. *Let's Take a Break: Exercise Poems for Young Children.* Continental Press, Elizabethtown, PA, 1981.

Huettig, C. *Gross Motor Activities for Classroom Educators of Children with Special Needs.* Dallas Independent School District, Dallas, TX, 1992.

Pyfer, J. *Motor Development Evaluation and Programming,* Texas Woman's University, Denton, TX, 1986.

Schurr, E. *Movement Experiences for Children: A Humanistic Approach to Elementary School Physical Education.* Englewood Cliffs, NJ: Prentice-Hall, 1980.

Warren, J. *1-2-3 Games: No-Lose Group Games for Young Children.* Everett, WA: Warren Publishing, 1986.

Young, S. B. *Movement is Fun: A Preschool Movement Program.* Torrance, CA: Sensory Integration International Publishers, 1988.